Teaching Notes

Contents

Introduction   2
Vocabulary chart   4
Curriculum coverage chart   5

Locked Out

Reading   6
Speaking and listening   8
Writing   8

Little Dragon

Reading   9
Speaking and listening   11
Writing   11

Alf Saves the Day

Reading   12
Speaking and listening   14
Writing   14

The School Trip

Reading   15
Speaking and listening   17
Writing   17

The Chatterbox Turtle

Reading   18
Speaking and listening   20
Writing   20

The Sandwich that Jack Made

Reading   21
Speaking and listening   23
Writing   23

Oxford Reading Tree resources at this level 24

Introduction

The *Snapdragons* series is a rich mix of different kinds of stories presented as picture books with expertly written text carefully levelled to provide reading practice at each stage in Key Stage 1.

This set of six books at Stage 5 provides practice in the early reading skills that children need to become competent readers. These stories introduce children to early key words as well as useful vocabulary relating to the different contexts. The longer books at Stage 5 will help children to build up stamina in their reading.

The six books include stories based in familiar settings which reflect everyday life, and the readers will quickly identify with the family members, school friends and pets, and recognise their experiences. There are also stories about fantasy worlds including animal fantasy tales, a traditional story from another culture, and a new rhyming story with a patterned and predictable structure, told in the traditional style of a familiar nursery rhyme.

Children are encouraged to look at the illustrations for visual cues to the words in the text, and to find out what is happening in the story. The picture book presentation will also encourage children to tell the story in their own words so that they develop their oral skills.

How to introduce the books

Before reading the story for guided or independent reading, always read the title and talk about the picture on the cover.

Go through the book together, looking at the pictures and talking about them. If there are context words (listed in the chart on page 4) that are new or unfamiliar, point them out and read them with the children. Read the story to the children, encouraging confident children to join in with you.

This booklet provides prompts and suggestions for using the books in groups and for guided, group and independent activities, matched to text, sentence and word level objectives. There are also separate Guided Reading Cards available for six titles at each stage. Suggestions are also provided for speaking and listening activities, writing activities, and cross-curricular links. You can use these suggestions to follow on from your reading or at another time.

Reading notes are also provided in each book. They can be found on the inside front and back covers of each book. These suggest friendly prompts and activities for parents or carers reading with their children at home.

Reading skills

Stage 5 develops:
- wider opportunities for independent reading
- a greater degree of self-support
- knowledge that new words can be formed from known words
- insights into a different style of story
- strategies for checking that reading makes sense
- reading stamina
- growing confidence in creative writing, particularly through the stimulus of the magic key.

Vocabulary chart

Stage 5		
Locked Out	Year 1 High Frequency Words	again back but came can't do door first gave girl got help her home house last laugh not one push ran school that then there to us very were what when where
	Context words	asleep babies barked biscuit Boxer clever flap Gran hug hungry key locked lucky opened pocket Suzie thank tired through try windows
Little Dragon	Year 1 High Frequency Words	blue brown call(ed) came can't do did have her if laugh(ed) little not one out school so their too very were will your
	Context words	breathe clapped claws didn't dragon fast(er) fire fly(ing) grew grow heavy land learned moo puffed roar(ed) sad sky teach(er) tried wings
Alf Saves the Day	Year 1 High Frequency Words	about after be boy(s) but five girl(s) good jump(ed) just loved mad next one people school some there too took want(ed) very what with were
	Context words	Alf cheered children coach drawing dribbling fan football goalkeep lady match(es) other passing picked pictures sad save shooting shot shouted stories team television watching writing
The School Trip	Year 1 High Frequency Words	after back but by came did didn't do don't first girl good got have help her here last little made much name next not our ran saw school so that their them then there too took us want(ed) very wa were your
	Context words	Aneesa animals bus chook cross duck farm(er) fed feed geese Greenwood Hilldown hands hen(s) hold horse(s) lamb(s) let lot lunc meet Mr Bell Mrs Hood noise pond Poppy ride run(ning) shoo shout sign Star teacher time Tom trip wash week
The Chatterbox Turtle	Year 1 High Frequency Words	about as back been blue but by came can't could do(ing) don't down got has here him his home if just laugh(ed) live(d) love(d) more must(n't) not now one our over put saw them their there time too two us want(ed) way were what where will with your
	Context words	animals ask(ed) beaks bet bump carry chatterbox closed drink fall f fell flew fly(ing) geese grinned held hold keep lake monkeys mout muddy parrots paws pool remember(ed) rushed say shout(ed) sky stick stop talk(ing) trees Turtle waved why wish word
The Sandwich that Jack Made	Year 1 High Frequency Words	but green here more over put red some then took yellow
	Context words	added bread butter cheese chips covered cream crispy dips dripping felt found Jack jar juicy lettuce lots mixed nice packet peas pot ric sick spice spread thick tomatoes top

Curriculum coverage chart

Stage 5	Speaking and listening	Reading	Writing
Locked Out			
NLS/SLL	Y1T2 5, 8	T5, S5, W2	T13, W1, W7
Scotland	Level A	Level A	Level A
N. Ireland	Activities: a, b, c Outcomes: a, b, d, e	Activities: a, b, c, e Outcomes: b, c, d, e, f	Outcomes: a, b, c, f, h
Wales	Range: 1, 2, 5, 6 Skills: 1, 2, 3, 4, 5, 6	Range: 1, 2, 4, 5, 6 Skills: 1, 2	Range: 1, 2, 3, 7 Skills: 1, 2, 3, 6, 7, 8
Little Dragon			
NLS/SLL	Y1T1 3, Y1T3 11	T5, S4, W3, W6, W8	T13, W7
Scotland	Level A	Level A	Level A
N. Ireland	Activities: a, f, d Outcomes: a, b, c, d, i	Activities: a, b, c Outcomes: b, c, d, e, f	Outcomes: a, b, c, h, i
Wales	Range: 1, 2, 3 Skills: 1, 2, 3, 4, 5, 6	Range: 1, 2, 4, 5, 6 Skills: 1, 2	Range: 1, 2, 3, 7 Skills: 1, 2, 3, 7, 8
Alf Saves the Day			
NLS/SLL	Y1T3 9	T3, S4, W6	T12, T13, W7
Scotland	Level A	Level A	Level A
N. Ireland	Activities: a, h Outcomes: c, d, f, g	Activities: a, b, c Outcomes: b, c, d, e, f	Outcomes: a, b, c, h, i
Wales	Range: 1 Skills: 1, 2	Range: 1, 2, 5, 6 Skills: 1, 2	Range: 1, 2, 3, 6, 7 Skills: 1, 3, 7, 8
The School Trip			
NLS/SLL	Y1T1 4, Y1T3 12	T18, S5, W5, W10	T20, W1, W7
Scotland	Level A	Level A	Level A
N. Ireland	Activities: a, b, c Outcomes: a, b, d, i	Activities: a, b, e Outcomes: b, c, d, e, f	Outcomes: a, b, c, e, h
Wales	Range: 1, 2, 5, 6 Skills: 1, 2, 3, 5	Range: 1, 2, 5, 6 Skills: 1, 2	Range: 1, 2, 3, 4, 7 Skills: 1, 3, 4, 5, 7, 8
The Chatterbox Turtle			
NLS/SLL	Y1T3 9	T3, S7, W6	T12, T13, W7
Scotland	Level A	Level A	Level A
N. Ireland	Activities: a, b, c Outcomes: b, c, d, i	Activities: a, b, c Outcomes: b, c, d, e, f	Outcomes: a, b, c, h
Wales	Range: 1, 2, 3, 5 Skills: 1, 2, 5	Range: 1, 2, 5, 6 Skills: 1, 2	Range: 1, 2, 3, 7 Skills: 1, 2, 3, 4, 7, 8
The Sandwich that Jack Made			
NLS/SLL	Y1T2 5, 7	T3, S3, W4	T2, T14
Scotland	Level A	Level A	Level A
N. Ireland	Activities: a, e Outcomes: b, c, d, e	Activities: a, b, e Outcomes: b, c, d, e, f	Outcomes: a, b, c, h
Wales	Range: 1, 2 Skills: 1, 2, 3	Range: 1, 2, 4, 5, 6 Skills: 1, 2	Range: 1, 2, 3, 4, 6, 7 Skills: 1, 3, 5, 7, 8

Locked Out

Reading the story

Introducing the story

- Read the title to the children. Ask them to predict what the problem might be in this book, and how it might be solved.
- Ask the children if they have been locked out themselves.
- Tell the children that the girl is called Suzie. Encourage them to tell the story as they look through the pages.

During reading

- Ask the children to read the story. Praise and encourage them as they read.
- If they find "Boxer" difficult, cover "er" and ask them to sound out "box", and then add the ending. Help the children to read "through" and "tired" if necessary and ask them to re-read and check that these words make sense.

Observing Check that the children:
- can read on sight familiar high frequency words
- use all searchlight information to decipher unknown vocabulary.

Group and independent reading activities

Text level work

Range familiar setting/predictable and patterned language

Objective To re-tell stories, to give the main points in sequence and to pick out significant incidents (T5).

- Ask the children to take turns to re-tell each part of the story in their own words, using the illustrations as a guide.
- Prompt and praise them for talking about the feelings of the two main characters e.g. ask: *How do you think Gran felt when she couldn't find her key?*

Observing Can the children describe the events coherently? Are they able to use their own experience to interpret the character's feelings?

Sentence level work

Objective To learn common uses of capitalisation (S5).

- On page 2, ask the children to identify the capital letters, and revise the use of capital letters at the beginning of sentences.
- Discuss the use of capital letters at the beginning of names, and ask the children if there is more than one reason for the capitals on page 2.
- Ask the children to comment on the use of capital letters on pages 3, 4, 9 and 10.

Observing Were the children able to use appropriate terms e.g. "capital letter", "sentence", "a person's name"? Were they able to explain why there were sometimes two reasons for a capital letter?

Word level work

Objective To read on sight high frequency words specific to graded books matched to the abilities of reading groups (W2).

You will need the following word cards:
  school, were, home, when, her, one, got, but, do, help, can't, not, girl, very, too, back, push
plus any YR words in the text that the children need to practise, e.g. said, out, they, was, you, get.

- Lay the cards out face-up.
- Ask the children in turn to read and pick up as many words as they can read accurately.
- Carry out extra practice on those words all children have difficulty with, e.g. ask them to count the letters; to sound them out slowly if appropriate; to make links with other words (to/do, put/push/pull); or to find smaller words within the words (on/one, hen/when).

Observing Do the children pay attention and learn while others are taking their turn? Are the children developing their own ways of remembering new words?

Speaking and listening activities

Objectives To explore familiar themes and characters through improvisation and role-play (Y1T2 5); To act out own and well known stories, using different voices for characters (Y1T2 8).

- Divide the children into two groups. Ask a child in each group to play the part of Gran, Suzie and Boxer, and a narrator if you wish.
- Ask each group to act out the story in turn, creating their own dialogue and extending the storyline.
- Discuss how their versions are different from the story in the book.

◀▶ **Cross-curricular link**
PSHE: family and friends should care for each other

Writing

Objectives To write about significant incidents from known stories (T13); To segment words into phonemes for spelling (W1); To spell common irregular words from Appendix List 1 (W7).

- Draw a stick figure in a coat with lots of pockets on the whiteboard, label it "Gran", and draw a speech bubble.
- Ask the children to discuss what Gran said when she couldn't find her key. Select one of the sentences and scribe it inside the speech bubble with the children.
- Repeat using a picture of Suzie crawling through the dog flap.

Little Dragon
Reading the story

Introducing the story
- Discuss the cover and read the title.
- Tell the children that Little Dragon went to a special Dragon School. Ask them what young dragons might have to learn.
- Ask the children to look through the book to check their predictions.

During reading
- As the children read the story, comment on the illustrations as they relate to the text.
- Support the children with the pronunciation of "breathe" and "heavy" by asking them to start sounding through the word as they think about its meaning.
- Praise the children for correcting their own reading. Suggest they re-read a passage if they lose the meaning or fluency.

Observing Check that the children:
- use an awareness of grammar to decipher verbs such as "grow" and "grew", "fly" and "flew"
- use a range of strategies to make sense of what they read.

Group and independent reading activities

Text level work
Range fantasy/predictable and patterned language

Objective To re-tell stories, to give the main points in sequence and to pick out significant incidents (T5).

You will need strips of card.
- Ask the group to re-tell the story, taking turns to add one part at a time.
- Scribe each section of the story on a separate strip of card with the children.

- Shuffle and lay out the cards. Ask the group to read and re-order them to follow the story sequence.

Observing Are the children able to recall the sequence accurately? Do they retain some of the literary phrases in their re-telling?

Sentence level work

Objectives To learn about word-order, e.g. by re-ordering sentences, grouping a range of words that might "fit" (S4); To learn new words from reading and shared experiences (W8).

- Write the following incomplete sentences and words on the board:
  The young dragons _____ fast.
  One dragon didn't _____ fast.
  grow, grew; flew, fly; ran, run
- Ask the children to read the sentences and the first pair of words below. Explain that they must choose "grow" or "grew" to fit the spaces.
- Discuss the different spellings of the pairs of words.
- Tell them that they need to listen to their own reading and check that it sounds like a person talking. Repeat with the remaining words.

Observing Are the children able to self-monitor?

Word level work

Objectives To read on sight other familiar words (W3); To investigate and learn spellings of verbs with "ed" (past tense), and "ing" (present tense) endings (W6).

- Tell the children that they are going to be word detectives. They will search for all the words in the book ending in "–ed".
- List the words on the whiteboard as the children locate them. ("learned", "called", "opened", "laughed", "liked", "puffed", "flapped", "tried", "roared", "breathed", "clapped" "smiled")
- Discuss and write the same root words with "–ing" endings.

How quickly can the children locate and read correctly appropriate words in the text?

Speaking and listening activities

Objectives To ask and answer questions, make relevant contributions, offer suggestions and take turns (Y1T1 3); To explain their views to others in a small group, and decide how to report the group's views to the class (Y1T3 11).

- Ask the children to take turns to summarise the story. Ask them to select one person to report to the class.
- Ask the children what the Big Dragons said about Little Dragon's attempts to roar and breathe fire, and her flying success.
- Ask the children to select a member of the group to talk about each part of the story.
- Let the children present their report to the rest of the class.

◄► **Cross-curricular link**
PSHE: developing confidence and making the most of their abilities

Writing

Objectives To write about significant incidents from known stories (T13); To write common irregular words from Appendix List 1 (W7).

- Ask the children to re-read pages 17–23, and talk about what happened when Little Dragon tried to fly. Encourage them to write about what Little Dragon did and how she felt.
- Work with individual children. Ask them to construct and repeat each sentence before writing, and monitor their own writing, re-reading where necessary.
- Ask the children to illustrate their stories.

Alf Saves the Day

Reading the story

Introducing the story

- Tell the children that the boy on the cover is Alf, and ask what they think the story will be about.
- Discuss what is meant by the expression "Saves the Day". (Comes to the rescue.)
- Look through the book, discussing aspects of football (e.g. watching, dribbling).

During reading

- Read the title with the children. Praise them for checking the illustrations before they read each page for themselves.
- Encourage them to start reading words such as p2 "everything" and p6 "matches", pointing out familiar parts of the words.
- Model expressive reading of the dialogue, making full use of the punctuation including exclamation marks.

Observing Check that the children
- read the high frequency words confidently
- expect reading to make sense and check if it does not
- use a range of strategies to decipher new words
- use the title and pictures to predict the content.

Group and independent reading activities

Text level work

Range familiar setting/predictable and patterned language

Objective To notice the difference between spoken and written forms through re-telling known stories (T3).

- On pages 16, 19 and 20, ask the children to describe what happened, e.g. p 16 "Alf told the children to look out." p19 "Everyone said it was a good save." p20 "The coach asked Alf to go with him." Scribe what they say.

- Ask the children to read their sentences and to go back to find the relevant parts of the story. Ask them to read them out, e.g. p16 *Suddenly Alf shouted, "Look out!"*
- Talk about the differences between the two ways of writing the same part of the story. Revise the use of speech marks.

Observing Were all the children able to locate the relevant part of the story? How well could they explain the use of direct speech?

Sentence level work

Objective To learn about word order, e.g. by re-ordering sentences (S4).

You will need the following word cards:
at, school, lots, of, children, played, football

- Lay out the cards in a random order and ask all the children to read them.
- Ask one child to put them in order to make a sentence. Scribe the sentence, asking the children which letter requires a capital, and what should go at the end.
- Ask other children to re-order the sentence, and scribe again, e.g. "Lots of children played football at school." "Children played lots of football at school."

Observing Do the children re-read each sentence carefully after assembling them?

Word level work

Objective To investigate and learn spellings of verbs with "ed" (past tense), "ing" (present tense) endings (W6).

- Tell the children that they are going to be detectives. Ask them to locate all the words in the story ending in "–ed" and "–ing".
- Write each word on a piece of card:
  loved, cheered, played, wanted, picked, shouted, jumped, saved drawing, writing, watching, going, dribbling, passing, shooting, heading
- Ask the children to re-arrange them into two columns and re-read.

- Ask the children to practise spelling the words using Look, Cover, Write and Check.

Observing Are the children able to focus on the ends of the words and categorise them quickly?

Speaking and listening activities

Objective To interpret a text by reading aloud with some variety of pace and emphasis (Y1T3 9).

- Read pages 2–5, modelling expressive reading aloud, with the children following the text as you read.
- Ask the children to take turns to read two pages each, pausing between phrases and emphasising key words.
- On pages 18 and 19, ask each child to read different sections of the text and speech bubbles.
- Model how to read the sentences on page 22. Point out that "And" is used to begin the second sentence to give it emphasis.

◀▶ **Cross-curricular links**
PE: explore basic skills, actions and ideas with increasing understanding
PSHE: make the most of their abilities

Writing

Objectives Through shared and guided writing to apply phonological, graphic knowledge and sight vocabulary to spell accurately (T12); To write about significant incidents from known stories (T13); To spell common irregular words from Appendix List 1 (W7).

- Ask the children which part of the story they like best. Make sure they talk about Alf's feelings.
- Encourage them to write down that part of the story, and why they like it.
- Help individuals to compose their ideas and sound out unknown words.

The School Trip

Reading the story

Introducing the story

- Tell the children that Tom wrote this story about his school trip to a farm. Ask them which animals Tom might see.
- As they look through the book, introduce the main characters: Mr Bell, Mrs Hood, and Aneesa.
- Talk together about the illustrations and help the children read the signs.

During reading

- Praise and encourage the children as they read.
- Draw attention to familiar elements in words, e.g. Hood/good; chook/look; Hill/down.
- On page 6, ask: *How would Mr Bell sound when he was cross?*
- On page 14, prompt the children to respond to larger type.
- Prompt the children to read the speech bubbles expressively.

Observing Check that the children:

- ■ read on sight high frequency words and other familiar words
- ■ recognise words by common spelling patterns
- ■ use awareness of grammar to decipher unfamiliar words
- ■ use a range of strategies to make sense of what they read
- ■ read the text aloud with pace and expression.

Group and independent reading activities

Text level work

Range familiar setting/predictable and patterned language

Objective To read recounts and begin to recognise generic structure, e.g. ordered sequence of events (T18).

- Discuss the term "recount". Explain how a recount is usually a true story that tells us **when**, **where** and **how** things happened.

- On page 2, ask the children to find when this story began ("Last week"), where ("a farm") and how ("on a bus").
- On page 6, talk about how the word "first" tells us that several things are going to happen.
- On pages 10, 14 and 17, ask the children to find the words that tell us about when other things happened. ("next", "then")
- Ask: *How does this recount finish? Why does Tom say that they made a lot of noise on the bus?*

Observing Do the children understand what is meant by a "recount"? Do they know which words show that time is passing?

Sentence level work

Objective To learn other common uses of capitalisation, e.g. for personal titles, headings, book titles, emphasis (S5).

- Ask the children to be text detectives and find capital letters in the story. Remind them of the uses of capitals.
- Write the headings below on a whiteboard. Ask the children to take turns to find capital letters on each page and to write them in the correct column, e.g.

Page number	Name	Sentence beginning
2	M B T M B	O L W W T M T

- Ask the children to continue as a group or on their own.

Observing Can the children quickly identify the different uses of capitals? Do they recognise that sometimes letters can be in both columns (e.g. "M" on page 8)?

Word level work

Objectives To recognise words by common spelling patterns (W5); To practise handwriting in conjunction with spelling and independent writing (W10).

- Ask the children to think of words that rhyme with "by" and "my".
- Scribe the children's suggestions, e.g. fly, try, sky, fry, spy, cry, dry, why.

- Ask the children to add rhyming words to the following pairs of words: "came"/"name"; "took"/"chook"; "lot"/"not".
- Ask the children to write and then read their lists.

Observing Are the children able to generate rhyming words? Can they spell and then read them correctly?

Speaking and listening activities

Objectives To explore familiar themes and characters through improvisation and role-play (Y1T1 4); To discuss why they like a performance (Y1T3 12).

You will need dressing-up clothes for Mrs Hood (the farmer) and Mr Bell (the teacher).

- Tell the children they are going to act out the story as a play.
- Choose children to play the parts of the farmer, teacher, Tom and Aneesa. The other children can join in as classmates, animals and the bus driver.
- Ask them to change roles. Praise realistic dialogue and convincing role-play.
- Ask for the children's opinions on who gave especially good performances.

◀▶ **Cross-curricular link**
Science: about living things and their habitats

Writing

Objectives To write simple recounts linked to topics of interest/study or to personal experience (T20); To segment words into phonemes for spelling (W1); To spell common irregular words from Appendix List 1 (W7).

- Discuss a recent event the children have experienced as a group or individually.
- Explain that they are going to write about it. Draw their attention to sequence words, such as "first", "next", "at last".
- Support individuals and encourage them to monitor their own work.

The Chatterbox Turtle

Reading the story

Introducing the story

- Read the title and ask the children what "Chatterbox" means. Say: *Turtle tried not to talk all the time but it was very hard for him. Let's see what happens.*
- Discuss the illustrations. Ask the children: *Why is it dangerous for Turtle to talk while he's in the air?*

During reading

- Praise individual children as they read. Prompt them to think about the story as they sound out unfamiliar words.
- Draw attention to question and exclamation marks, and ask children to re-read to achieve richer expressiveness.
- On page 15, break "remembered" into syllables if necessary. (re/mem/bered).

Observing Check that the children:

- use a range of strategies to work out new words
- expect reading to make sense and check if it does not
- read on sight high frequency words.

Group and independent reading activities

Text level work

Range fantasy/traditional story/from another culture

Objective To notice the difference between spoken and written forms through re-telling known stories (T3).

You will need the following sentence strips:
Turtle talked to animals at the muddy pool.
The geese said they live far away.
Turtle wanted to go to the beautiful lake.
Up flew the geese with Turtle holding the stick.

Snake teased Turtle and he opened his mouth.
Down fell Turtle, but he was all right.

- Put the strips in random order and ask each child to read one of the sentences. Discuss with the group how to place the strips in the correct sequence.
- Re-read the strips to make a complete story.

Observing Are the children able to recall the story sequence? Do they re-read and refer to the text when necessary?

Sentence level work

Objective To add question marks to questions (S7).

- Write the following sentences on the whiteboard:
  Turtle will fall if he talks.
  "You are going to the lake, Turtle."
  He was all right.
  "You can't stop talking."

- Re-read the questions on pages 4 and 7, noting the question marks.
- Ask the children to read the statements on the whiteboard. Show them how to reword the first to make a question, and add punctuation. ("Will Turtle fall if he talks?")
- Scribe with the children, changing the statements into questions, and asking them to add the punctuation. Read the new questions together.

Observing Do the children understand how to change the wording to construct questions?

Word level work

Objective To investigate and learn spellings of verbs with "ed" (past tense), "ing" (present tense) endings (W6).

- Ask children to locate verbs ending in "–ed" in the text, and list them on the whiteboard. (lived, loved, asked, looked, waved, shouted, wanted, remembered, laughed, rushed, grinned)

- Ask the children to remove "–ed" and add "-ing" to each word. Ask them to write the words on paper or a whiteboard. In pairs, let them take turns to read each other's lists.

Observing Do the children remember to remove "–ed" each time, and re-read what they have written?

Speaking and listening activities

Objective To interpret a text by reading aloud with some variety in pace and emphasis (Y1T3 9).

- Tell the children that they are going to read the story as though it was a play. Select children to take the part of Turtle, geese, parrots, monkeys, Snake and narrator.
- Remind them that speech marks show the words the characters say. Experiment with suitable voices for the different animals.
- Perform the story with animal masks for the rest of the class.

◀▶ **Cross-curricular link**
Creative development: exploring colour, texture and shape by making animal masks; use in role play

Writing

Objectives Through shared and guided writing to apply phonological, graphic knowledge and sight vocabulary to spell words accurately (T12); To write about significant incidents from known stories (T13); To spell common irregular words from Appendix List 1 (W7).

- Ask the children to talk about their favourite part of the story and draw it. While they are drawing, discuss with each child two or three sentences they are going to write underneath.
- Remind the children to re-read their work and to keep track of the story. Praise lively language and independent attempts to spell unknown words.
- Allow time for each child to read his or her story to others in the group.

The Sandwich that Jack Made

Reading the story

Introducing the story

- Read the title. Ask children to predict how the author might write a whole book about a sandwich. Write down ideas and suggestions about how the book might end.
- Do the children think the sandwich looks good to eat?

During reading

- Ask the children to read the story after examining the illustrations on each spread.
- Ensure children are phrasing well. Explain that they need to read a phrase fluently, and take a pause before the next phrase, e.g. p10 "on top of the butter/Jack spread on the bread".
- If children find it difficult to track the lines of print, e.g. on p14 or p21, suggest they place an index finger at the end of the line they are reading.

Observing Check that the children:
- apply their word-level skills in guided reading
- read the text aloud with pace and expression appropriate to the grammar.

Group and independent reading activities

Text level work

Range familiar setting/new spin on traditional story/rhyme with patterned and predictable structure

Objective To notice the difference between spoken and written forms through re-telling known stories; compare oral versions with the written text (T3).

- Discuss elements of this text that make it different from others, and record the discussion in the children's words, e.g.

When something is added, the whole text is repeated.	In most stories, the author would just say what Jack did next.
Each new filling is made up of words that rhyme.	The filling would be something people would really like to eat.
The text is more like a poem because it sort of gallops along.	Sentences in normal stories sound more like talking.
It's not like real life – more like a fantasy.	Most stories would be about normal things you put in sandwiches.

Observing Are the children able to express their ideas clearly? Are they able to give examples from the text?

Sentence level work

Objective To learn about word order, e.g. by predicting words from previous text (S3).

- **You will need** the following phrases on cards:

  Jack put in some rice   and added some spice
  Jack found some chips   and a packet of dips
  He added the peas   and some of the cheese
  Here is the butter he spread   on the bread

- Jumble up the eight strips and ask the children to read the words and fit the sentences together properly.
- Ask children to put them in the order introduced in the story, and then re-read together.

Observing Do the children make use of the rhyming pairs to make the sentences? Did they refer to the text when putting them in order?

Word level work

Objective To read on sight more high frequency words from Appendix List 1 (W4).

- Write these words on the whiteboard: here, some, then, put, over, with, found.

- Ask the children to go through the text, making a checklist of the number of times each word appears.
- Have a quick spelling test.

Observing Can the children scan the text to locate the words quickly? Do they work page by page or take each word in turn?

Speaking and listening activities

Objectives To retell stories, using events using story language (Y1T2 5); To take turns to speak, listen to others' suggestions and talk about what they are going to do (Y1T2 7).

- Tell the children that they are going to retell this story as a narrative, taking turns to describe what happened. Encourage them to add details of their own, e.g. *It was a very wet day and Jack couldn't think of anything to do. Then he had an idea.* Or *Jack was starving. His mum was still out shopping and he just couldn't wait any longer for lunch.*
- Encourage the children to listen to each other's ideas and keep their own contributions brief. Praise imaginative thinking and language.

◀▶ **Cross-curricular link**
PSHE: recognising what they like and dislike.

Writing

Objectives To use phonological, contextual, grammatical and graphic knowledge to work out, and check the meanings of unfamiliar words (T2); To write stories using simple settings (T14).

- Ask the children to write their own version, e.g. *The Sandwich that Imran/Yanifa Made.* Remind them to re-read their sentences in order to keep track of their story line.
- Clap the syllables of longer words to help with spelling.
- Let the children illustrate and publish their stories.

Oxford Reading Tree resources at this level

There is a range of material available at a similar level to these stories which can be used for consolidation or extension.

Stage 5

Teacher support
- Teacher's Handbook
- Big Book for Stage 5 Stories
- Guided Reading Cards for Stage 5 Stories
- Take-Home Card for each story
- Extended Stories
- Storytapes / More Storytapes
- Context Cards
- Workbooks 5a and 5b
- Woodpeckers Photocopy Masters
- Group Activity Sheets Book 2 Stages 4 & 5
- ORT Games Stages 4 & 5

Further reading
- Oxford Reading Tree Storybooks for Core Reading
- Stage 5 Playscripts
- Woodpeckers Phonics Anthology 1
- Branch Library Victor Books Pack A
- Story Rhymes
- Fireflies Non-Fiction
- Fact Finders Units B and C
- Glow-worms Poetry

Electronic
- Clip Art
- Stage 5 Talking Stories
- ORT Online www.OxfordReadingTree.com
- Floppy and Friends

For developing phonics
- Alphabet frieze, Tabletop Alphabet Mats, Alphabet Photocopy Masters
- Card Games
- First Story Rhymes

OXFORD
UNIVERSITY PRESS

Great Clarendon Street, Oxford OX2 6DP

Oxford University Press is a department of the University of Oxford. It furthers the University's objective of excellence in research, scholarship, and education by publishing worldwide in

Oxford   New York

Auckland   Cape Town   Dar es Salaam   Hong Kong   Karachi Kuala Lumpur   Madrid   Melbourne   Mexico City   Nairobi New Delhi   Shanghai   Taipei   Toronto

With offices in

Argentina   Austria   Brazil   Chile   Czech Republic   France Greece   Guatemala   Hungary   Italy   Japan   Poland   Portugal Singapore   South Korea   Switzerland   Thailand   Turkey Ukraine   Vietnam

Oxford is a registered trade mark of Oxford University Press in the UK and in certain other countries

The moral rights of the author have been asserted

Database right Oxford University Press (maker)

First published 2005

British Library Cataloguing in Publication Data

Data available

Cover illustrations by Chris Mould

Teacher's Notes: ISBN 978-0-19-845543-1

10 9 8

Page make-up by Fakenham Photosetting, Fakenham, Norfolk

Printed in China by imago